CAMPFIRE
COOKING

Publications International, Ltd.

WARNING: Food preparation, baking and cooking involve inherent dangers: misuse of electric products, sharp electric tools, boiling water, hot stoves, allergic reactions, foodborne illnesses and the like, pose numerous potential risks. Publications International, Ltd. (PIL) assumes no responsibility or liability for any damages you may experience as a result of following recipes, instructions, tips or advice in this publication.

While we hope this publication helps you find new ways to eat delicious foods, you may not always achieve the results desired due to variations in ingredients, cooking temperatures, typos, errors, omissions, or individual cooking abilities.

Acknowledgments
The publisher would like to thank the companies listed below for the use of their recipes and photographs in this publication.

McCormick®

Recipes Courtesy of the Reynolds Kitchens

CONTENTS

Biscuit-Wrapped Sausages (page 7)

Bratwurst Skillet Breakfast (page 14)

French Toast Kabobs (page

4

Toad in a Hole (page 10)

Classic Hash Browns (page 21)

DAYBREAK DELIGHTS

Twisted Cinnamon Biscuits (page 22)

BISCUIT-WRAPPED SAUSAGES
MAKES 12 SERVINGS

1 can (8 ounces) refrigerated crescent roll dough
1 package (12 count) fully cooked breakfast sausage links
Maple syrup

1 Cut each dough sheet into 1-inch strips; roll each strip into 6-inch rope. Skewer sausages onto long roasting skewers or clean sticks; wrap with dough. Hold over medium coals of campfire. Cook and turn 6 minutes or until golden brown.

2 Remove to heatproof surface. Cool slightly; remove to large serving platter. Serve with maple syrup.

BREAKFAST MIGAS
MAKES 6 SERVINGS

1 small ripe avocado, diced

1 tablespoon lime juice

6 eggs

2 tablespoons chunky salsa

1 tablespoon olive oil

1 small onion, chopped

1 jalapeño pepper,* seeded and diced

3 corn tortillas, cut into 1-inch pieces

1 medium tomato, halved, seeded and diced

1 cup (4 ounces) shredded Monterey Jack cheese

Sour cream and sprigs fresh cilantro (optional)

Jalapeño peppers can sting and irritate the skin, so wear rubber gloves when handling peppers and do not touch your eyes.

1 Preheat grilling grid over campfire. Combine avocado and lime juice in medium bowl; toss to coat. Lightly whisk eggs and salsa in medium bowl until blended.

2 Heat oil in large cast iron skillet over medium coals. Add onion and jalapeño pepper; cook and stir 1 minute or until softened. Add tortillas and tomato; cook 2 minutes or until tortillas are softened and heated through.

3 Pour egg mixture into skillet; cook until eggs are firmly scrambled, stirring occasionally. Remove skillet from grid; stir in cheese. Top migas with avocado; serve with sour cream and cilantro, if desired.

NOTE

Migas, a Mexican breakfast dish, is traditionally made with leftover, stale tortillas that are torn by hand into small pieces.

TOAD IN A HOLE
MAKES 1 SERVING

2 slices sandwich bread

1 slice cheese

2 tablespoons butter, divided

2 sausage links, sliced in half

1 egg

Salt and black pepper

1 Cut circle in center of both bread slices and cheese; discard centers or reserve for another use. Layer 1 tablespoon butter, bread slice, cheese, sausage links (around edge of bread) and remaining bread slice in pie iron. Crack egg in center of sandwich; top with 1 tablespoon butter. Sprinkle egg with salt and pepper.

2 Hold pie iron level over medium coals of campfire 6 minutes or until golden brown on each side, turning once. Remove to heatproof surface; carefully remove sandwich to serving plate.

BREAKFAST BISCUIT BAKE
MAKES 8 SERVINGS

8 ounces bacon, chopped

1 small onion, finely chopped

1 clove garlic, minced

¼ teaspoon red pepper flakes

5 eggs

¼ cup milk

½ cup (2 ounces) shredded white Cheddar cheese, divided

¼ teaspoon salt

⅛ teaspoon black pepper

1 package (16 ounces) refrigerated jumbo buttermilk biscuits (8 biscuits)

1 Preheat grilling grid over campfire. Cook bacon in large cast iron skillet over medium coals until crisp. Remove bacon to paper towel-lined plate. Drain off and reserve drippings, leaving 1 tablespoon in skillet.

2 Add onion, garlic and red pepper flakes to skillet; cook and stir 8 minutes or until onion is softened. Set aside to cool slightly.

3 Whisk eggs, milk, ¼ cup cheese, salt and black pepper in medium bowl until well blended. Stir in onion mixture.

4 Wipe out any onion mixture remaining in skillet; grease with additional drippings, if necessary. Separate biscuits and arrange in single layer in bottom of skillet. (Bottom of skillet should be completely covered.) Pour egg mixture over biscuits; sprinkle with remaining ¼ cup cheese and cooked bacon.

5 Cook over medium coals 10 minutes or until puffed and golden brown. Serve warm.

BRATWURST SKILLET BREAKFAST
MAKES 4 SERVINGS

3 bratwurst links (about ¾ pound), cut into ¼-inch-thick slices

2 tablespoons butter

1½ pounds red potatoes, cut into ¼- to ½-inch pieces

1½ teaspoons caraway seeds

4 cups shredded red cabbage

1 Preheat grilling grid over campfire.

2 Cook bratwurst in large cast iron skillet over medium coals 8 minutes or until browned and cooked through. Transfer to paper towel. Pour off drippings.

3 Melt butter in same skillet. Add potatoes and caraway seeds; cook 10 to 12 minutes or until potatoes are golden and tender, stirring occasionally. Return bratwurst to skillet; stir in cabbage. Cook, covered, 3 minutes or until cabbage is slightly wilted. Uncover; cook and stir 3 to 4 minutes or until cabbage is just tender.

DAYBREAK DELIGHTS

STUFFED FRENCH TOAST SANDWICH

MAKES 1 SERVING

2 tablespoons butter

2 slices whole wheat or white bread

1 thin slice deli ham (about 1 ounce)

1 egg

3 tablespoons milk

1 teaspoon sugar

Maple syrup, warmed

Sliced fresh strawberries and oranges (optional)

1 Layer 1 tablespoon butter, 1 slice bread, ham, 1 slice bread and 1 tablespoon butter in pie iron.

2 Whisk egg, milk and sugar in small bowl. Pour egg mixture over sandwich. Close pie iron.

3 Hold pie iron level over medium coals of campfire 6 minutes or until golden brown on each side, turning once. Remove to heatproof surface; carefully remove sandwich to serving plate. Serve sandwich with maple syrup and fruit, if desired.

CRISPY SKILLET POTATOES

MAKES 4 SERVINGS

2 tablespoons olive oil

4 red potatoes, cut into thin wedges

½ cup chopped onion

2 tablespoons lemon-pepper seasoning

½ teaspoon coarse salt

Chopped fresh parsley (optional)

1 Preheat grilling grid over campfire.

2 Heat oil in large cast iron skillet over medium coals. Stir in potatoes, onion, lemon-pepper seasoning and salt. Cover; cook 10 to 15 minutes or until potatoes are tender and browned, turning occasionally.

3 Sprinkle with parsley just before serving, if desired.

FRENCH TOAST KABOBS

MAKES 4 SERVINGS

1 cup milk

2 eggs

3 tablespoons granulated sugar

2 teaspoons vanilla

⅛ teaspoon salt

8 slices French bread (about 1 inch thick, 2½ to 3 inches in diameter)

¾ cup tangerine juice or orange juice

¼ cup honey

2 teaspoons cornstarch

¼ teaspoon ground ginger or ground cinnamon

Powdered sugar (optional)

1 cup fresh raspberries (optional)

1 Spray grilling grid with nonstick cooking spray. Preheat grid over campfire. Soak four 12-inch wooden skewers in water while preparing bread.

2 Beat milk, eggs, granulated sugar, vanilla and salt in shallow dish until well blended. Place bread slices in egg mixture. Let stand 5 minutes, turning to soak all sides.

3 Meanwhile, heat tangerine juice, honey, cornstarch and ginger in small cast iron saucepan over medium coals. Bring to a boil, stirring constantly. Cook and stir 1 minute. Remove from heat; cover to keep warm.

4 Thread 4 pieces bread onto each prepared skewer. Cook 4 to 5 inches from medium coals 3 to 5 minutes or until lightly browned. Turn skewers; cook 3 to 5 minutes or until lightly browned.

5 Spoon juice mixture onto plates; top with kabobs. Sprinkle with powdered sugar and raspberries, if desired. Serve immediately.

APPLE CINNAMON GRILL

MAKES 1 SERVING

2 slices cinnamon raisin bread

1 tablespoon cream cheese

3 thin slices Granny Smith apple

Dash ground cinnamon

1 tablespoon red raspberry or any flavor preserves

2 tablespoons butter

1 Spread 1 slice bread with cream cheese; top with apple slices and cinnamon. Spread remaining bread slice with preserves; place on top of apples to create sandwich. Place 1 tablespoon butter, sandwich and 1 tablespoon butter in pie iron; close pie iron.

2 Hold pie iron over medium coals of campfire 6 minutes or until golden brown on each side, turning once. Remove to heatproof surface; carefully remove sandwich to serving plate.

CLASSIC HASH BROWNS
MAKES 2 SERVINGS

1 large russet potato,
    peeled and grated

¼ teaspoon salt

⅛ teaspoon black pepper

2 tablespoons vegetable
    oil

1 Preheat grilling grid over campfire. Heat medium cast iron skillet over medium coals 5 minutes. Combine potato, salt and pepper in small bowl; toss to coat.

2 Add oil to skillet; heat 30 seconds. Spread potato mixture evenly in skillet. Cook about 5 minutes without stirring or until bottom is browned. Turn potatoes; cook 5 minutes or until golden brown and crispy.

TWISTED CINNAMON BISCUITS
MAKES 12 SERVINGS

1 cup granulated sugar

3 tablespoons ground cinnamon

1 can (8 ounces) refrigerated crescent roll dough

½ cup (1 stick) butter, melted

1 Combine sugar and cinnamon in small bowl; stir to blend. Set aside. Cut each dough sheet into 1-inch strips; roll each strip into 6-inch rope. Twist dough around long roasting skewers or clean sticks. Toast over medium coals of campfire. Cook and turn 6 minutes or until lightly browned.

2 Remove biscuits onto heatproof surface. Cool slightly; remove to large plate. Brush with melted butter and sprinkle with cinnamon-sugar mixture.

WHOLE WHEAT PANCAKES

MAKES 4 SERVINGS (ABOUT 12 PANCAKES)

¾ cup milk

2 eggs

¼ cup plain Greek yogurt

2 tablespoons vegetable oil

1 tablespoon honey

1 cup whole wheat flour

2 teaspoons baking powder

⅛ teaspoon salt

2 teaspoons butter

Fresh raspberries, blueberries and/or strawberries (optional)

Maple syrup (optional)

1 Preheat grilling grid over campfire.

2 Whisk milk, eggs, yogurt, oil and honey in medium bowl until well blended. Add flour, baking powder and salt; whisk just until blended.

3 Heat large cast iron skillet over medium coals. Add 1 teaspoon butter; brush to evenly coat skillet. Drop batter by ¼ cupfuls into skillet. Cook 2 minutes or until tops of pancakes appear dull and bubbles form around edges. Turn and cook 1 to 2 minutes or until firm and bottoms are browned, adding remaining 1 teaspoon butter as needed. Top with berries and maple syrup, if desired.

SAUSAGE AND CHEDDAR CORN BREAD
MAKES 10 SERVINGS

1 tablespoon vegetable oil

½ pound bulk pork sausage

1 medium onion, diced

1 jalapeño pepper,* diced

1 package (8 ounces) corn muffin mix

1 cup (4 ounces) shredded Cheddar cheese, divided

⅓ cup milk

1 egg

Jalapeño peppers can sting and irritate the skin, so wear rubber gloves when handling peppers and do not touch your eyes.

1 Preheat grilling grid over campfire.

2 Heat oil in large cast iron skillet over medium coals. Brown sausage 6 to 8 minutes, stirring to break up meat. Add onion and jalapeño pepper; cook and stir 5 minutes or until vegetables are softened. Remove sausage mixture to medium bowl.

3 Combine corn muffin mix, ½ cup cheese, milk and egg in separate medium bowl. Pour batter into skillet. Spread sausage mixture over top. Sprinkle with remaining ½ cup cheese. Cover; cook over medium coals 15 to 20 minutes or until edges are lightly browned. Cut into wedges to serve.

SWEET POTATO AND TURKEY SAUSAGE HASH

MAKES 2 SERVINGS

1 tablespoon vegetable oil, divided

1 mild or hot turkey Italian sausage link (about 4 ounces), casing removed

1 small red onion, finely chopped

1 small red bell pepper, finely chopped

1 medium sweet potato, peeled and cut into ½-inch cubes

¼ teaspoon salt

¼ teaspoon black pepper

⅛ teaspoon ground cumin

⅛ teaspoon chipotle chili powder

1 Preheat grilling grid over campfire.

2 Heat 1½ teaspoons oil in large cast iron skillet over medium coals. Brown sausage 3 to 5 minutes, stirring to break up meat into ½-inch pieces. Remove sausage to plate.

3 Heat remaining 1½ teaspoons oil in same skillet. Add onion, bell pepper, sweet potato, salt, black pepper, cumin and chili powder; cook and stir 5 to 8 minutes or until sweet potato is tender.

4 Stir in sausage; cook without stirring 5 minutes or until hash is lightly browned.

SAWMILL BISCUITS AND GRAVY

MAKES 8 SERVINGS

3 tablespoons canola or vegetable oil, divided

8 ounces bulk breakfast sausage

2¼ cups plus 3 tablespoons biscuit baking mix, divided

2⅔ cups whole milk, divided

¼ teaspoon salt

¼ teaspoon black pepper

1 Preheat grilling grid over campfire.

2 Heat 1 tablespoon oil in large cast iron skillet over medium coals. Add sausage; cook and stir 6 to 8 minutes or until browned, stirring to break up meat. Remove to medium bowl using slotted spoon.

3 Add remaining 2 tablespoons oil to skillet. Add 3 tablespoons biscuit mix; whisk until smooth. Gradually add 2 cups milk; cook and stir 3 to 4 minutes or until mixture comes to a boil. Cook and stir 1 minute or until thickened. Add sausage and any juices; cook and stir 2 minutes. Season with salt and pepper.

4 Combine remaining 2¼ cups biscuit mix and ⅔ cup milk in medium bowl; stir until blended. Spoon batter into eight mounds onto gravy mixture. Cover; cook 10 to 15 minutes or until biscuits are golden.

CHORIZO HASH

MAKES 4 SERVINGS

2 unpeeled russet potatoes, cut into ½-inch pieces

1 tablespoon salt, divided

8 ounces Mexican chorizo sausage

1 yellow onion, chopped

½ red bell pepper, chopped

Fried or poached eggs (optional)

Avocado slices (optional)

Fresh cilantro leaves (optional)

1 Preheat grilling grid over campfire.

2 Fill medium saucepan half full with water. Add potatoes and 2 teaspoons salt; bring to a boil over high heat. Reduce heat to medium-low; cook about 8 minutes. (Potatoes will be firm.) Drain.

3 Meanwhile, remove and discard casing from chorizo. Crumble chorizo into large cast iron skillet; cook and stir over medium-high heat about 5 minutes or until lightly browned. Add onion and bell pepper; cook and stir about 4 minutes or until vegetables are softened.

4 Stir in potatoes and remaining 1 teaspoon salt; cook 10 to 15 minutes or until vegetables are tender and potatoes are lightly browned, stirring occasionally. Serve with eggs, avocado and cilantro, if desired.

Campfire BBQ Burgers (page 52)

Grilled Buffalo Chicken Wraps (page 58)

Southwestern Chicken Soup (page 50)

Pepperoni Pizza Sandwich (page 37)

BOWLS AND SANDWICHES

...orn Chip Chili (page 38)

Bratwurst Sandwiches (page 48)

PEPPERONI PIZZA SANDWICH

MAKES 1 SERVING

2 slices white sandwich bread

2 tablespoons prepared pizza sauce

3 tablespoons mozzarella cheese

5 slices pepperoni

2 tablespoons butter

1 Spread 1 slice bread with pizza sauce; top with cheese, pepperoni and 1 slice bread. Place 1 tablespoon butter in pie iron. Add sandwich; top with 1 tablespoon butter. Close pie iron.

2 Hold pie iron level over medium coals of campfire 6 minutes or until golden brown on each side, turning once. Remove to heatproof surface; carefully remove sandwich to serving plate.

TOASTED CHEESE SANDWICH

Layer 1 tablespoon butter, 1 slice bread, your favorite cheese(s), 1 slice bread and 1 tablespoon butter in pie iron. Close pie iron. Follow method step 2 as directed above. Makes 1 serving.

CORN CHIP CHILI

MAKES 6 SERVINGS

1 tablespoon olive oil

1 medium onion, chopped

1 medium red bell pepper, chopped

1 jalapeno pepper,* seeded and finely chopped

4 cloves garlic, minced

2 pounds ground beef

1 can (4 ounces) diced green chiles, drained

2 cans (about 14 ounces each) fire-roasted diced tomatoes

2 tablespoons chili powder

1½ teaspoons ground cumin

1½ teaspoons dried oregano

¾ teaspoon salt

3 cups corn chips

1 cup (4 ounces) shredded sharp Cheddar cheese

6 tablespoons chopped green onions

*Jalapeño peppers can sting and irritate the skin, so wear rubber gloves when handling peppers and do not touch your eyes.

1 Place grilling grid over campfire. Heat oil in Dutch oven over medium coals. Add onion, bell pepper, jalapeño pepper and garlic; cook and stir 2 minutes or until softened. Add beef; cook and stir 10 to 12 minutes or until beef is no longer pink and liquid has evaporated. Stir in green chiles; cook 1 minute. Stir in tomatoes, chili powder, cumin and oregano.

2 Cover; cook 30 minutes or until heated through. Stir in salt. Place corn chips evenly into serving bowls; top with chili. Sprinkle with cheese and green onions.

MEATY CHILI DOGS

MAKES 12 SERVINGS

1 pound ground beef

¼ pound Italian sausage, casings removed

1 large onion, chopped

2 medium stalks celery, diced

1 jalapeño pepper,* seeded and chopped

2 cloves garlic, minced

1 tablespoon chili powder

2 teaspoons sugar

1 can (28 ounces) diced tomatoes

1 can (about 15 ounces) pinto beans, rinsed and drained

1 can (12 ounces) tomato juice

1 cup water

12 hot dogs

12 hot dogs buns, split

Jalapeño peppers can sting and irritate the skin, so wear rubber gloves when handling peppers and do not touch your eyes.

1 Preheat grilling grid over campfire.

2 Cook beef, sausage, onion, celery, jalapeño pepper and garlic in Dutch oven over medium coals until meat is cooked through and onion is tender, stirring to break up meat. Drain fat.

3 Stir in chili powder and sugar. Add tomatoes, beans, tomato juice and water. Simmer 30 minutes, stirring occasionally.

4 Arrange hot dogs on grid directly above medium coals. Grill 5 to 8 minutes or until heated through, turning often. Place hot dogs in buns; top each hot dog with about ¼ cup chili.

HEARTY BEEFY BEER SOUP

MAKES 6 SERVINGS

1 tablespoon vegetable oil

¾ pound boneless beef round steak, cut into ½-inch pieces

1 large onion, chopped

2 medium carrots, sliced

2 stalks celery, diced

5 cups beef broth

1 bottle (12 ounces) stout or dark ale

¾ teaspoon dried oregano

¼ teaspoon salt

⅛ teaspoon black pepper

1 can (about 15 ounces) kidney beans, rinsed and drained

1 small zucchini, cut into ½-inch cubes

4 ounces mushrooms, sliced

1 Preheat grilling grid over campfire.

2 Heat oil in Dutch oven over medium coals. Add beef, onion, carrots and celery; cook and stir 6 to 8 minutes or until beef is no longer pink and carrots and celery are crisp-tender.

3 Stir in broth, stout, oregano, salt and pepper. Simmer, uncovered, 45 minutes or until beef is fork-tender.

4 Stir in beans, zucchini and mushrooms. Simmer, uncovered, 5 minutes or until zucchini is tender.

BACON AND TOMATO MELTS

MAKES 4 SANDWICHES

Nonstick cooking spray

8 slices bacon, crisp-cooked

8 slices (1 ounce each) Cheddar cheese

2 tomatoes, sliced

8 slices whole wheat bread

¼ cup (½ stick) butter, melted

1 Spray grilling grid with cooking spray. Preheat grid over campfire.

2 Layer 2 slices bacon, 2 slices cheese and tomato slices on each of 4 bread slices; top with remaining bread slices. Brush sandwiches with butter.

3 Place sandwiches on grid; press lightly with spatula or weigh down with small plate. Cook over medium coals 4 to 5 minutes per side or until cheese melts and sandwiches are golden brown.

CLASSIC CHILI

MAKES 6 SERVINGS

1½ pounds ground beef

1½ cups chopped onion

1 cup chopped green bell pepper

2 cloves garlic, minced

3 cans (about 15 ounces each) dark red kidney beans, rinsed and drained

2 cans (about 15 ounces each) tomato sauce

1 can (about 14 ounces) diced tomatoes

2 to 3 teaspoons chili powder

1 to 2 teaspoons dry hot mustard

¾ teaspoon dried basil

½ teaspoon black pepper

1 to 2 dried hot chile peppers (optional)

Shredded Cheddar cheese (optional)

1 Preheat grilling grid over campfire.

2 Combine beef, onion, bell pepper and garlic in Dutch oven; cook and stir over medium coals 6 to 8 minutes or until beef is browned and onion is tender. Drain fat.

3 Add beans, tomato sauce, diced tomatoes, chili powder, mustard, basil, black pepper and chile peppers, if desired, to Dutch oven; stir to blend. Cover and cook 1 hour. Remove and discard chiles before serving. Top with cheese, if desired.

BRATWURST SANDWICHES
MAKES 4 SERVINGS

4 bratwurst (about 1 pound)

1 bottle or can (12 ounces) beer

1 onion, sliced

1 red bell pepper, cut into thin strips

1 green bell pepper, cut into thin strips

1 tablespoon olive oil

¾ teaspoon salt

½ teaspoon black pepper

4 hoagie or submarine sandwich rolls, split

Spicy brown or Dijon mustard

Hot sport peppers (optional)

1 Preheat grilling grid over campfire.

2 Combine bratwurst and beer in cast iron skillet; bring to a simmer over medium coals. Simmer, uncovered, 10 to 15 minutes or until bratwurst are no longer pink in center, turning occasionally.

3 Combine onion and bell peppers on large sheet of heavy-duty foil. Drizzle with oil; season with salt and black pepper. Place another sheet of foil over vegetables; fold up all edges of foil, forming packet.

4 Place foil packet on grid; grill 5 minutes. Place bratwurst on grid; turn vegetable packet over. Continue grilling 10 minutes or until bratwurst are heated through and vegetables are tender, turning bratwurst and foil packet once.

5 Place rolls, split sides down, on grid to toast lightly during final minutes of grilling. Serve bratwurst and vegetables in rolls. Serve with mustard and hot peppers, if desired.

SOUTHWESTERN CHICKEN SOUP

MAKES 6 SERVINGS

½ teaspoon salt

¼ teaspoon black pepper

¼ teaspoon garlic powder

4 boneless skinless chicken breasts (about 1 pound)

1 tablespoon olive oil

1 medium onion, halved and sliced

1 small jalapeño pepper,* seeded and chopped (optional)

4 cans (about 14 ounces each) chicken broth

2 cups peeled and diced potatoes

2 small zucchini, sliced

1½ cups frozen corn

1 cup diced tomato

2 tablespoons lime or lemon juice

1 tablespoon chopped fresh cilantro

Corn bread (optional)

Jalapeño peppers can sting and irritate the skin, so wear rubber gloves when handling peppers and do not touch your eyes.

1 Preheat grilling grid over campfire. Combine salt, black pepper and garlic powder in small bowl; sprinkle evenly over chicken.

2 Heat oil in Dutch oven over medium coals. Add chicken; cook, without stirring, 2 minutes or until golden. Turn chicken; cook 2 minutes. Add onion and jalapeño pepper, if desired; cook 2 minutes.

3 Add broth; stir in potatoes. Simmer 5 minutes. Add zucchini, corn and tomato; cook 10 minutes or until tender. Stir in lime juice and cilantro just before serving. Serve with corn bread, if desired.

CAMPFIRE BBQ BURGERS

MAKES 6 SERVINGS

Nonstick cooking spray

1½ pounds ground beef

5 tablespoons barbecue sauce, divided

1 onion, cut into thick slices

1 tomato, sliced

2 tablespoons olive oil

6 Kaiser rolls, split

6 leaves green or red leaf lettuce

1 Spray grilling grid with cooking spray. Preheat grid over campfire.

2 Combine beef and 2 tablespoons barbecue sauce in large bowl. Shape into 6 (1-inch-thick) patties.

3 Grill patties over medium coals 13 to 15 minutes to medium (160°F) or to desired doneness, turning occasionally. Brush both sides with remaining 3 tablespoons barbecue sauce during last 5 minutes of cooking.

4 Meanwhile, brush onion and tomato slices with oil. Grill onion slices about 10 minutes and tomato slices 2 to 3 minutes.

5 Just before serving, place rolls, cut side down, on grid; grill until lightly toasted. Serve burgers on rolls with tomato, onion and lettuce.

TROPICAL TURKEY MELT
MAKES 1 SERVING

1 English muffin, split

1 teaspoon Dijon mustard

3 slices (about 3 ounces) deli smoked turkey

3 thin slices papaya

1 slice (1 ounce) Monterey Jack cheese

2 tablespoons butter

1 Spread inside of muffin halves with mustard. Layer turkey, papaya and cheese over one muffin half. Press remaining muffin half, mustard-side down, over cheese. Place 1 tablespoon butter, sandwich and 1 tablespoon butter in pie iron; close pie iron.

2 Hold pie iron over medium coals of campfire 6 minutes or until golden brown on each side, turning once. Remove to heatproof surface; carefully remove sandwich to serving plate.

BACON BURGERS

MAKES 4 SERVINGS

Nonstick cooking spray

8 slices bacon

4 pounds ground beef

1½ teaspoons chopped fresh thyme *or* ½ teaspoon dried thyme

½ teaspoon salt

Dash black pepper

4 slices Swiss cheese

4 Asiago rolls, split

1 Spray grilling grid with cooking spray. Preheat grid over campfire. Cook bacon in large cast iron skillet until crisp. Remove bacon from skillet; drain on paper towel-lined plate. Crumble 4 slices bacon.

2 Combine beef, crumbled bacon, thyme, salt and pepper in medium bowl; mix lightly. Shape into 4 patties.

3 Grill patties over medium coals, 8 to 10 minutes or until cooked through (160°F) or to desired doneness, turning occasionally. Top with cheese during last 2 minutes of grilling. Serve on rolls with remaining bacon slices; garnish as desired.

EASY VEGETABLE BEEF STEW

MAKES 4 SERVINGS

1 pound beef stew meat

1 can (about 14 ounces) diced tomatoes

1 onion, cut into 8 wedges

4 carrots, cut into 1-inch pieces

1 green or red bell pepper, diced

1 stalk celery, sliced

1 teaspoon Italian seasoning

½ teaspoon salt

½ teaspoon black pepper

1 tablespoon vegetable oil

1 package (8 ounces) sliced mushrooms

1 Preheat grilling grid over campfire.

2 Combine beef, tomatoes and onion in Dutch oven; cover and cook over medium coals 20 minutes. Stir in carrots, bell pepper, celery, Italian seasoning, salt and black pepper; cook 15 minutes or until beef and carrots are tender.

3 Heat oil in large cast iron skillet over medium coals. Add mushrooms; cook and stir 10 minutes or until lightly browned and tender. Stir mushrooms into stew.

VARIATION

Two unpeeled medium red potatoes, cut into 2-inch pieces, can be added with the carrots.

GRILLED BUFFALO CHICKEN WRAPS

MAKES 4 SERVINGS

4 boneless skinless
   chicken breasts
   (about 4 ounces each)

¼ cup plus 2 tablespoons
   buffalo wing sauce,
   divided

2 cups broccoli slaw

2 tablespoons blue cheese
   salad dressing

4 (8-inch) whole wheat
   tortillas, warmed

1 Place chicken in large resealable food storage bag. Add
   ¼ cup buffalo sauce; seal bag and turn to coat. Marinate
   in refrigerator or cooler 15 minutes.

2 Meanwhile, preheat grilling grid over campfire. Grill chicken
   over medium coals 5 to 6 minutes per side or until no longer
   pink. When cool enough to handle, slice chicken; combine
   with remaining 2 tablespoons buffalo sauce in medium bowl.

3 Combine broccoli slaw and blue cheese dressing in large bowl;
   mix well.

4 Arrange chicken and broccoli slaw down center of tortillas; roll
   up tightly to secure filling. Cut in half diagonally.

TIP
If you don't like the spicy flavor of
buffalo wing sauce, substitute your
favorite barbecue sauce.

CHICKEN NOODLE SOUP

MAKES 8 SERVINGS (10 CUPS)

2 tablespoons butter

1 cup chopped onion

1 cup sliced carrots

½ cup diced celery

2 tablespoons vegetable oil

1 pound boneless skinless chicken breasts

1 pound boneless skinless chicken thighs

4 cups chicken broth, divided

2 cups water

2 tablespoons chopped fresh parsley

1½ teaspoons salt

½ teaspoon black pepper

3 cups uncooked egg noodles

1 Preheat grilling grid over campfire.

2 Melt butter in Dutch oven over medium coals. Add onion, carrots and celery; cook 15 minutes or until vegetables are soft, stirring occasionally.

3 Meanwhile, heat oil in large cast iron skillet over medium coals. Add chicken; cook 12 minutes or until lightly browned and cooked through. Transfer chicken to large cutting board. Add 1 cup broth to skillet; cook 1 minute, scraping up any browned bits from bottom of skillet. Add broth to vegetables. Stir in remaining 3 cups broth, water, parsley, salt and pepper.

4 Chop chicken into 1-inch pieces when cool enough to handle. Add to soup; cook 15 minutes. Add noodles; cook 15 minutes or until noodles are tender.

GRILLED VEGETABLE MUFFALETTA

MAKES 6 SERVINGS

1 small eggplant, cut lengthwise into ⅛-inch slices

1 yellow squash, cut lengthwise into ⅛-inch slices

1 zucchini, cut on the diagonal into ⅛-inch slices

¼ cup extra virgin olive oil

½ teaspoon salt

¼ teaspoon black pepper

1 (8-inch) boule or round bread, cut in half horizontally

1 container (8 ounces) hummus, any flavor

1 jar (12 ounces) roasted red peppers, drained

1 jar (6 ounces) marinated artichoke hearts, drained and chopped

1 small tomato, thinly sliced

1 Preheat grilling grid over campfire.

2 Combine eggplant, squash, zucchini, oil, salt and pepper in large bowl; toss to coat. Grill vegetables over medium coals 2 to 3 minutes per side or until tender and golden brown. Cool to room temperature.

3 Scoop out bread from both halves of boule with your fingers, leaving about 1 inch of bread on edges and about 1½ inches on bottom. Spread hummus evenly on inside bottom of bread.

4 Layer grilled vegetables, roasted peppers, artichokes and tomato over hummus; cover with top half of bread. Wrap stuffed loaf tightly in plastic wrap. Chill sandwich in refrigerator or cooler at least 1 hour before cutting into wedges.

GRILLED BAJA BURRITOS

MAKES 4 SERVINGS

6 tablespoons vegetable oil, divided

3 tablespoons lime juice, divided

2 teaspoons chili powder

1½ teaspoons lemon-pepper seasoning

1 pound tilapia fillets

3 cups coleslaw mix

½ cup chopped fresh cilantro

¼ teaspoon salt

¼ teaspoon black pepper

Guacamole and pico de gallo (optional)

4 (7-inch) flour tortillas

Lime wedges (optional)

1 Preheat grilling grid over campfire. Combine 2 tablespoons oil, 1 tablespoon lime juice, chili powder and lemon-pepper seasoning in large resealable food storage bag. Add fish; seal bag and turn to coat. Let stand 10 minutes.

2 Brush grid with 2 tablespoons oil. Remove fish from marinade; discard marinade. Grill fish over medium coals 6 to 8 minutes or until center is opaque, carefully turning once.

3 Combine coleslaw mix, remaining 2 tablespoons oil, 2 tablespoons lime juice, cilantro, salt and pepper in medium bowl; mix well.

4 Layer fish, coleslaw mixture, guacamole and pico de gallo, if desired, on tortillas; roll up tightly to secure filling. Serve with additional pico de gallo and lime wedges, if desired.

TIP

If tilapia is not available, any firm white fish, such as snapper or halibut, can be used instead.

Beef and Vegetable Skewers (page 70)

Ginger Sesame Salmon Packets (page 84)

Cajun BBQ Beer Can Chicken (page 82)

...lking Tacos (page 80)

OUTDOOR DINNERS

All-American Barbecue
Grilled Chicken (page 75)

PIZZA CASSEROLE

MAKES 6 SERVINGS

1½ pounds ground beef

1 medium onion, chopped

Salt and black pepper

2 cups cooked rotini or other spiral pasta

1 can (about 15 ounces) pizza sauce

1 can (8 ounces) tomato sauce

1 can (6 ounces) tomato paste

½ teaspoon sugar

½ teaspoon garlic salt

½ teaspoon dried oregano

1 cup (4 ounces) shredded mozzarella cheese

12 to 15 slices pepperoni

1 Preheat grilling grid over campfire.

2 Heat large cast iron skillet over medium coals. Brown beef with onion in skillet 6 to 8 minutes, stirring to break up meat. Drain fat. Season with salt and pepper.

3 Stir in pasta, pizza sauce, tomato sauce, tomato paste, sugar, garlic salt and oregano; top with cheese and pepperoni slices. Cook 10 to 15 minutes or until heated through and cheese is melted.

BEEF AND VEGETABLE SKEWERS

MAKES 4 SERVINGS

2 pounds boneless sirloin steak, cut into 1½-inch pieces

¼ cup Italian salad dressing

2 tablespoons Worcestershire sauce

1 red bell pepper, cut into 12 pieces

1 green bell pepper, cut into 12 pieces

1 yellow bell pepper, cut into 12 pieces

1 zucchini, cut into 12 pieces

1 Place steak in medium bowl. Add dressing and Worcestershire sauce; stir to coat. Marinate in refrigerator or cooler 30 minutes. Soak eight bamboo skewers in water 20 minutes.

2 Oil grilling grid. Preheat grid over campfire. Alternately thread beef, bell peppers and zucchini onto skewers.

3 Grill skewers, covered, over medium coals 10 minutes or until beef is at least 145°F or until desired degree of doneness, turning occasionally.

SOUTHERN FRIED CATFISH WITH HUSH PUPPIES

MAKES 4 SERVINGS

Hush Puppy Batter (recipe follows)

4 catfish fillets (about 1½ pounds)

½ cup yellow cornmeal

3 tablespoons all-purpose flour

1½ teaspoons salt

¼ teaspoon ground red pepper

Vegetable oil for frying

Prepared tartar sauce (optional)

1 Preheat grilling grid over campfire. Prepare Hush Puppy Batter; set aside.

2 Rinse catfish; pat dry with paper towels. Combine cornmeal, flour, salt and ground red pepper in shallow dish. Coat fish with cornmeal mixture.

3 Pour oil into large cast iron skillet to depth of 1 inch; heat over medium coals to 375°F. Cook fish in batches 4 to 5 minutes or until golden brown and fish begins to flake when tested with fork. Drain fish on paper towels; keep warm. *Allow temperature of oil to return to 375°F between batches.*

4 Drop Hush Puppy Batter by tablespoonfuls into hot oil (oil should be 375°F); cook in batches 2 minutes or until golden brown. Drain on paper towel-lined plate. Serve with catfish and tartar sauce, if desired.

HUSH PUPPY BATTER
MAKES ABOUT 24 HUSH PUPPIES

1½ cups yellow cornmeal

½ cup all-purpose flour

2 teaspoons baking
powder

½ teaspoon salt

1 cup milk

1 small onion, minced

1 egg, lightly beaten

Combine cornmeal, flour, baking powder and salt in medium
bowl; stir to blend. Add milk, onion and egg; stir until well
blended. Allow batter to stand 5 to 10 minutes.

BEER GRILLED STEAKS
MAKES 4 SERVINGS

1 cup light-colored beer,
    such as lager

¼ cup soy sauce

2 tablespoons molasses

2 cloves garlic, minced

½ teaspoon salt

¼ teaspoon black pepper

4 beef rib-eye steaks,
    1 inch thick (4 to
    6 ounces each)

Nonstick cooking spray

1 Whisk beer, soy sauce, molasses, garlic, salt and pepper in small
  bowl. Place steaks in large resealable food storage bag; add
  beer mixture. Marinate in refrigerator or cooler at least 2 hours.

2 Spray grilling grid with cooking spray. Preheat grid over campfire.
  Grill steaks over medium coals, covered, 8 to 10 minutes per
  side until at least 145°F or until desired degree of doneness.

ALL-AMERICAN BARBECUE GRILLED CHICKEN

MAKES 4 SERVINGS

1 sheet REYNOLDS
    WRAP® Non-Stick Foil

6 chicken pieces

1 cup southwestern
    barbecue sauce

1 Heat grill to medium-high. Make drainage holes in sheet of REYNOLDS WRAP® Non-Stick Foil with a large fork. Place foil sheet on grill grate with non-stick (dull) side facing up; immediately place chicken on foil.

2 Grill covered 10 minutes. Turn chicken; brush chicken with barbecue sauce. Grill 10 minutes longer; turn chicken. Brush again with barbecue sauce; continue grilling until chicken is tender and reaches 180°F. Discard any remaining sauce.

SOUTHWESTERN BARBECUE SAUCE

Add 2 teaspoons chili powder, 1 teaspoon dry mustard, ¼ teaspoon garlic powder and ¼ teaspoon cayenne pepper to barbecue sauce. Grill as directed above.

75

FISH TACOS
MAKES 4 SERVINGS

1 pound skinless tilapia, mahi mahi or other firm white fish fillets

1 teaspoon chipotle hot pepper sauce, divided

1 teaspoon ground cumin

1 teaspoon garlic salt

2 teaspoons canola or vegetable oil

1 red bell pepper, cut into strips

1 green bell pepper, cut into strips

8 corn tortillas, warmed

4 limes, cut into wedges

Sour cream mixed with chopped fresh cilantro (optional)

1 Preheat grilling grid over campfire. Cut fish into 1-inch pieces; toss with ½ teaspoon hot pepper sauce, cumin and garlic salt in medium bowl.

2 Heat oil in large cast iron skillet over medium coals. Add fish; cook 3 to 4 minutes or until center is opaque, turning once. Remove to plate.

3 Add bell peppers to skillet; cook 6 to 8 minutes or until tender. Return fish to skillet. Add remaining ½ teaspoon hot pepper sauce; cook just until heated through.

4 Spoon mixture into tortillas. Serve with lime wedges and sour cream mixture, if desired.

BABY BACK BARBECUE RIBS

MAKES 5 TO 6 SERVINGS

2 sheets (18×24 inches each) REYNOLDS WRAP® Non-Stick Foil

3 pounds baby back pork ribs

1 tablespoon packed brown sugar

1 tablespoon paprika

2 teaspoons garlic powder

1½ teaspoons pepper

½ cup water or 6 to 8 ice cubes, divided

1½ cups barbecue sauce

1 Preheat grill to medium.

2 Center half of ribs on each sheet of REYNOLDS WRAP® Non-Stick Foil. Combine brown sugar and spices; rub over ribs, turning to coat evenly.

3 Bring up foil sides. Double fold top and one end to seal packet. Through open end, add ¼ cup of water or 3 to 4 ice cubes. Double fold remaining end, leaving room for heat circulation inside. Repeat to make two packets.

4 Grill for 45 to 60 minutes in covered grill. Remove ribs from foil; place ribs on grill.

5 Brush ribs with barbecue sauce. Continue grilling 10 to 15 minutes, brushing with sauce and turning every 5 minutes.

WALKING TACOS
MAKES 6 SERVINGS

3 medium plum tomatoes, chopped

2 tablespoons chopped onion

1 small jalapeño pepper,* seeded and minced

1 tablespoon chopped fresh cilantro

1 tablespoon lime juice

2 pounds ground beef

1 teaspoon salt

1 teaspoon garlic powder

1 teaspoon ground cumin

1 teaspoon paprika

1 teaspoon chili powder

½ teaspoon ground red pepper

½ teaspoon red pepper flakes

6 bags (2 ounces each) nacho-flavored chips

1 cup (4 ounces) shredded Mexican cheese blend

Jalapeño peppers can sting and irritate the skin, so wear rubber gloves when handling peppers and do not touch your eyes.

1 Preheat grilling grid over campfire. Combine tomatoes, onion, jalapeño pepper, cilantro and lime juice in medium bowl; mix well.

2 Brown beef in large cast iron skillet over medium coals 6 to 8 minutes, stirring to break up meat. Drain fat.

3 Stir in salt, garlic powder, cumin, paprika, chili powder, ground red pepper and red pepper flakes; cook 3 minutes or until heated through.

4 Open chip bags; fold sides around edges. Top chips with taco mixture; sprinkle with cheese and salsa.

CAJUN BBQ BEER CAN CHICKEN
MAKES 12 SERVINGS

4 (12-ounce) cans beer or non-alcoholic malt beverage

1½ cups **Cattlemen's®** Award Winning Classic Barbecue Sauce

¾ cup Cajun spice or Southwest seasoning blend

3 whole chickens (3 to 4 pounds each)

12 sprigs fresh thyme

CAJUN BBQ SAUCE

1 cup **Cattlemen's®** Award Winning Classic Barbecue Sauce

½ cup beer or non-alcoholic malt beverage

¼ cup butter

1 tablespoon Cajun spice or Southwest seasoning blend

1 Combine 1 can beer, 1½ cups barbecue sauce and ½ cup spice blend. Following manufacturer's instructions, fill marinade injection needle with marinade. Inject chickens in several places at least 1-inch deep. Place chickens into resealable plastic food storage bags. Pour any remaining marinade over chickens. Seal bag; marinate in refrigerator 1 to 3 hours or overnight.

2 Meanwhile, prepare Cajun BBQ Sauce: In saucepan, combine 1 cup barbecue sauce, ½ cup beer, butter and 1 tablespoon spice blend. Simmer 5 minutes. Refrigerate and warm just before serving.

3 Open remaining cans of beer. Spill out about ½ cup beer from each can. Using can opener, punch several holes in tops of cans. Spoon about 1 tablespoon additional spice blend and 4 sprigs thyme into each can. Place 1 can upright into each cavity of chicken, arranging legs forward so chicken stands upright.

4 Place chickens upright over indirect heat on barbecue grill. Cook on a covered grill on medium-high (350°F), about 1½ hours until thigh meat registers 180°F internal temperature. (Cover with foil if they become too brown while cooking.) Let stand 10 minutes before serving. Using tongs, carefully remove cans from chicken. Cut into quarters to serve. Serve with Cajun BBQ Sauce.

GINGER SESAME SALMON PACKETS

MAKES 4 SERVINGS

4 sheets (12×18 inches each) REYNOLDS WRAP® Non-Stick Foil

4 thin onion slices, separated into rings

2 medium carrots, cut into julienne strips or shredded

4 salmon fillets (4 to 6 ounces each)

2 teaspoons grated fresh ginger

2 tablespoons seasoned rice vinegar

1 teaspoon sesame oil

Salt and pepper

Fresh spinach leaves

1 Preheat grill to medium-high.

2 Center one-fourth of onion slices and carrots on each sheet of REYNOLDS WRAP® Non-Stick Foil with non-stick (dull) side toward food. Top with salmon. Sprinkle with ginger; drizzle with rice vinegar and sesame oil. Sprinkle with salt and pepper to taste.

3 Bring up foil sides. Double fold top and ends to seal packet, leaving room for heat circulation inside. Repeat to make four packets.

4 Grill 14 to 18 minutes in covered grill. Serve salmon and vegetables on a bed of spinach. Sprinkle with additional seasoned rice vinegar, if desired.

FAJITAS
MAKES 6 SERVINGS

¼ cup corn or vegetable oil

⅓ cup fresh lime juice
(from 2 or 3 limes)

½ package (about
2 tablespoons) fajita
seasoning mix

1 pound boneless chicken
or pork, chopped into
1-inch pieces

½ white or red onion,
sliced lengthwise

½ green bell pepper,
sliced lengthwise

½ red bell pepper,
sliced lengthwise

Flour tortillas, warmed

Optional toppings:
shredded Cheddar
cheese, sprigs fresh
cilantro, sliced
avocado, diced
tomatoes and/or
salsa (optional)

1 Combine oil, lime juice and fajita seasoning mix in large resealable food storage bag; mix well. Add chicken; seal bag and turn to coat. Marinate in refrigerator or cooler 1 hour.

2 Preheat grilling grid over campfire. Remove chicken from marinade; discard marinade.

3 Heat large cast iron skillet over medium coals. Add drained chicken, onion and bell peppers; cook and stir 6 to 8 minutes or until chicken is no longer pink and vegetables are tender.

4 Spoon mixture into warm tortillas; top as desired.

HAM AND BARBECUED BEAN SKILLET

MAKES 4 SERVINGS

1 tablespoon vegetable oil

1 cup chopped onion

1 teaspoon minced garlic

1 can (about 15 ounces) kidney beans, rinsed and drained

1 can (about 15 ounces) cannellini or Great Northern beans, rinsed and drained

1 cup chopped green bell pepper

½ cup packed brown sugar

½ cup ketchup

2 tablespoons cider vinegar

2 teaspoons dry mustard

1 ham steak (½ inch thick, about 12 ounces), cut into ½-inch pieces

1 Preheat grilling grid over campfire.

2 Heat oil in large cast iron skillet over medium coals. Add onion and garlic; cook and stir 3 minutes. Add beans, bell pepper, brown sugar, ketchup, vinegar and mustard; stir to blend.

3 Add ham to skillet. Reduce heat to low. Simmer 5 minutes or until sauce thickens and mixture is heated through, stirring occasionally.

BARBECUE PORK KABOBS
MAKES 4 SERVINGS

½ cup ketchup

¼ cup white vinegar

¼ cup vegetable oil

1 tablespoon packed brown sugar

1 teaspoon dry mustard

1 clove garlic *or* ½ teaspoon garlic powder

½ teaspoon salt

½ teaspoon Worcestershire sauce

¼ teaspoon black pepper

¼ teaspoon hot pepper sauce (optional)

4 boneless pork chops, cut into 1½-inch cubes

2 green bell peppers, cut into chunks

2 onions, cut into chunks

Red beans and rice (optional)

1 Combine ketchup, vinegar, oil, brown sugar, dry mustard, garlic, salt, Worcestershire sauce, black pepper and hot pepper sauce, if desired, in large resealable food storage bag; mix well. Reserve ¼ cup marinade for basting. Add pork; seal bag and turn to coat. Marinate in refrigerator or cooler at least 1 hour.

2 Preheat grilling grid over campfire.

3 Remove pork from marinade; discard marinade. Alternately thread pork, bell peppers and onions onto skewers.

4 Grill skewers over medium coals 15 to 20 minutes or until pork is barely pink in center, turning once and basting often with reserved ¼ cup marinade. *Do not baste during last 5 minutes of cooking.* Discard any remaining marinade. Serve with red beans and rice, if desired.

SAUSAGE AND PEPPERS

MAKES 4 SERVINGS

1 pound uncooked hot or mild Italian sausage links

2 tablespoons olive oil

3 medium onions, cut into ½-inch slices

2 red bell peppers, cut into ½-inch slices

2 green bell peppers, cut into ½-inch slices

1½ teaspoons coarse salt, divided

1 teaspoon dried oregano

Italian rolls (optional)

1 Preheat grilling grid over campfire. Fill large cast iron skillet half full with water. Add sausage; cook 5 minutes over medium coals. Drain sausage; cut diagonally into 1-inch slices.

2 Heat oil in same skillet. Add sausage; cook 10 minutes or until browned, stirring occasionally. Remove to plate; set aside.

3 Add onions, bell peppers, 1 teaspoon salt and oregano to skillet; cook over medium heat 30 minutes or until vegetables are very soft and browned in spots, stirring occasionally.

4 Stir sausage and remaining ½ teaspoon salt into skillet; cook 3 minutes or until heated through. Serve with rolls, if desired.

NUTTY PAN-FRIED TROUT

MAKES 4 SERVINGS

2 tablespoons olive oil

½ cup seasoned dry bread crumbs

4 trout fillets (about 6 ounces each)

½ cup pine nuts

1 Preheat grilling grid over campfire.

2 Heat oil in large cast iron skillet over medium coals. Place bread crumbs on plate. Coat fish with bread crumbs.

3 Add fish to skillet; cook 4 minutes per side or until fish begins to flake when tested with fork. Transfer to plate; keep warm.

4 Add pine nuts to drippings in skillet; cook and stir 3 minutes or until nuts are lightly toasted. Sprinkle over fish.

OUTDOOR DINNERS

MEXICAN CASSEROLE WITH TORTILLA CHIPS

MAKES 4 SERVINGS

1 tablespoon vegetable oil

12 ounces ground turkey

1 can (about 14 ounces) stewed tomatoes

½ (16-ounce) package frozen bell pepper stir-fry blend, thawed

¾ teaspoon ground cumin

½ teaspoon salt

½ cup (2 ounces) shredded sharp Cheddar cheese

2 ounces tortilla chips, broken into pieces

1 Preheat grilling grid over campfire.

2 Heat oil in large cast iron skillet over medium coals. Add turkey; cook until until no longer pink, stirring to break up meat. Stir in tomatoes, bell peppers, cumin and salt; bring to a boil. Reduce heat to low; cover and cook 15 minutes or until vegetables are tender.

3 Sprinkle with cheese and chips just before serving.

CHICKEN AND FRUIT KABOBS

MAKES 6 SERVINGS

¾ cup honey

6 tablespoons lemon juice

¼ cup Dijon mustard

3 tablespoons minced
fresh ginger

2 pounds boneless skinless
chicken breasts, cut
into 1-inch pieces

3 fresh plums, pitted
and quartered

2 firm bananas, cut
into chunks

2 cups fresh pineapple
chunks

1 Oil grilling grid. Preheat grid over campfire. Soak 12 wooden skewers in water 20 minutes.

2 Combine honey, lemon juice, mustard and ginger in small bowl; mix well. Alternately thread chicken chicken and fruit onto skewers; brush generously with honey mixture.

3 Grill kabobs over medium coals 5 minutes per side, brushing frequently with honey mixture. Grill 10 minutes more or until chicken is cooked through, turning and brushing frequently with remaining honey mixture.

BBQ CHICKEN SKILLET PIZZA

MAKES 4 TO 6 SERVINGS

1 pound frozen bread dough, thawed

1 tablespoon olive oil

2 cups shredded cooked chicken

¾ cup barbecue sauce, divided

¼ cup (1 ounce) shredded mozzarella cheese

¼ cup thinly sliced red onion

½ cup (2 ounces) shredded smoked Gouda

Chopped fresh cilantro (optional)

1 Preheat grilling grid over campfire.

2 Roll out dough into 15-inch circle on lightly oiled or floured surface. Brush oil over bottom and side of large cast iron skillet; place skillet over medium coals 5 minutes to preheat.

3 Combine chicken and ½ cup barbecue sauce in medium bowl; mix well. Remove hot skillet from campfire; press dough into bottom and about 1 inch up side of skillet.

4 Spread remaining ¼ cup barbecue sauce over dough. Sprinkle with mozzarella; top with chicken mixture. Sprinkle with half of onion and Gouda cheese; top with remaining onion.

5 Cook over medium coals about 25 minutes or until crust is golden brown. Sprinkle with cilantro, if desired.

Skillet Mac and Cheese (page 112)

Buffalo Onions (page 114)

Bacon-Wrapped Roasted Corn (page 105)

Fire-Roasted Hasselback
Potatoes (page 106)

SIZZLIN' SIDES

Basil Biscuits (page 120)

sted Sweet Potatoes (page 124)

BACON-WRAPPED ROASTED CORN
MAKES 4 SERVINGS

2 tablespoons butter, softened

2 teaspoons lemon juice

½ teaspoon salt

4 ears corn, husks and silks removed

4 slices bacon

1 Preheat grilling grid over campfire.

2 Combine butter, lemon juice and salt in small bowl. Brush mixture evenly over corn; wrap each ear with bacon.

3 Place four sheets of foil (about 6×9 inches each) on work surface; center ear of corn on each piece of foil. Bring up sides of foil; fold over top and edges to seal.

4 Grill packets over medium coals, covered, 15 minutes or until corn is tender, turning once.

FIRE-ROASTED HASSELBACK POTATOES

MAKES 6 SERVINGS

6 large baking potatoes

Olive oil

2 tablespoons garlic powder

1 tablespoon salt

2 teaspoons black pepper

1 Cut potatoes crosswise into ¼-inch-thick sections, leaving about ¼ inch uncut at bottom.

2 Rub each potato with oil, garlic powder, salt and pepper, making sure oil and seasonings get inside potato slices. Place each potato on 12×6-inch piece of foil. Roll up loosely to seal.

3 Place potatoes around edge of campfire directly on medium coals. Cook 40 minutes or until potatoes are softened. Remove to heatproof surface using large tongs. Let stand until potatoes are cool enough to handle.

TANGY RED CABBAGE WITH APPLES AND BACON

MAKES 4 SERVINGS

8 slices thick-cut bacon

1 large onion, sliced

½ small head red cabbage (1 pound), thinly sliced

1 tablespoon sugar

1 Granny Smith apple, peeled and sliced

2 tablespoons cider vinegar

½ teaspoon salt

¼ teaspoon black pepper

1 Preheat grilling grid over campfire.

2 Cook bacon in large cast iron skillet over medium coals 6 to 8 minutes or until crisp, turning occasionally. Drain on paper towel-lined plate. Coarsely chop bacon.

3 Drain all but 2 tablespoons drippings from skillet. Add onion; cook and stir over 2 to 3 minutes or until onion begins to soften. Add cabbage and sugar; cook and stir 4 to 5 minutes or until cabbage wilts. Stir in apple; cook 3 minutes or until crisp-tender. Stir in vinegar; cook 1 minute or until absorbed.

4 Stir in bacon, salt and pepper; cook 1 minute or until heated through. Serve warm or at room temperature.

BALSAMIC BUTTERNUT SQUASH

MAKES 4 SERVINGS

3 tablespoons olive oil

2 tablespoons thinly sliced fresh sage (about 6 large leaves), divided

1 medium butternut squash, peeled and cut into 1-inch pieces (4 to 5 cups)

½ red onion, cut in half then cut into ¼-inch slices

1 teaspoon salt, divided

2½ tablespoons balsamic vinegar

¼ teaspoon black pepper

1 Preheat grilling grid over campfire.

2 Heat oil in large cast iron skillet over medium coals. Add 1 tablespoon sage; cook and stir 3 minutes. Add squash, onion and ½ teaspoon salt; cook 6 minutes, stirring occasionally. Cook 5 minutes without stirring.

3 Stir in vinegar, remaining ½ teaspoon salt and pepper; cook 5 minutes or until squash is tender, stirring occasionally. Stir in remaining 1 tablespoon sage; cook 1 minute.

SKILLET MAC AND CHEESE

MAKES 6 SERVINGS

8 ounces thick-cut bacon, cut into ½-inch pieces

¼ cup finely chopped onion

¼ cup all-purpose flour

3½ cups whole milk

1 cup (4 ounces) shredded white Cheddar cheese

1 cup (4 ounces) shredded fontina cheese

1 cup (4 ounces) shredded Gruyère cheese

¾ cup grated Parmesan cheese, divided

½ teaspoon salt

½ teaspoon dry mustard

¼ teaspoon ground red pepper

¼ teaspoon black pepper

1 pound cavatappi or rotini pasta, cooked and drained

¼ cup panko bread crumbs

1 Preheat grilling grid over campfire.

2 Cook bacon in large cast iron skillet over medium coals until crisp; drain on paper towel-lined plate.

3 Add onion to drippings in skillet; cook and stir 4 minutes or until translucent. Add flour; cook and stir 5 minutes. Slowly add milk over medium-low heat, stirring constantly. Stir in Cheddar, fontina, Gruyère, ½ cup Parmesan, salt, mustard, ground red pepper and black pepper until smooth and well blended. Add cooked pasta; stir gently until coated. Stir in bacon.

4 Combine panko and remaining ¼ cup Parmesan in small bowl; sprinkle over pasta. Cook 30 minutes or until sauce has thickened and pasta is heated through.

BUFFALO ONIONS
MAKES 6 SIDE-DISH SERVINGS

½ cup **FRANK'S® RedHot®** Original Cayenne Pepper Sauce

½ cup (1 stick) butter *or* margarine, melted *or* olive oil

¼ cup barbecue sauce

1 tablespoon chili powder (optional)

4 large sweet onions, cut into ½-inch-thick slices

WHISK together **FRANK'S® RedHot®** Original Cayenne Pepper Sauce, butter, barbecue sauce and chili powder in medium bowl until blended; brush on onion slices.

GRILL onions over medium heat 10 minutes or until tender, turning and brushing frequently with **FRANK'S® RedHot®** mixture.

TIPS

Onions may be prepared ahead and grilled just before serving.

To make Grilled Buffalo Garlic Bread, combine *¼ cup each* **FRANK'S® RedHot®** Sauce and melted butter with *1 teaspoon* minced garlic. Lightly brush on thick slices of Italian bread. Grill or toast until golden. Top with blue cheese crumbles, if desired.

GARDEN VEGETABLE PACKET

MAKES 4 TO 6 SERVINGS

1 sheet (18×24 inches)
REYNOLDS WRAP®
Heavy Duty Aluminum
Foil

3 cups broccoli florets

2 cups cauliflower florets

½ medium red bell pepper,
cut into 1-inch pieces

1 teaspoon dried basil

½ teaspoon salt

⅛ teaspoon pepper

2 ice cubes

1 Preheat grill to medium-high.

2 Center broccoli, cauliflower and red pepper on sheet of
REYNOLDS WRAP® Heavy Duty Aluminum Foil. Sprinkle
with basil, salt and pepper. Top with ice cubes.

3 Bring up foil sides. Double fold top and ends to seal making
one large foil packet, leaving room for heat circulation inside.

4 Grill 15 to 18 minutes in covered grill.

SPICY ASIAN GREEN BEANS
MAKES 4 SERVINGS

1 pound whole green beans, trimmed

2 tablespoons chopped green onions

2 tablespoons dry sherry or chicken broth

4½ teaspoons soy sauce

1 teaspoon chili sauce with garlic

1 teaspoon dark sesame oil

1 clove garlic, minced

1 Preheat grilling grid over campfire.

2 Fill Dutch oven with water to depth of ½ inch; bring to a boil over medium coals. Place green beans in steamer basket in Dutch oven. Cover and steam 5 minutes or just until crisp-tender. Drain and set aside.

3 Combine green onions, sherry, soy sauce, chili sauce, sesame oil and garlic in small bowl. Spray Dutch oven with nonstick cooking spray; heat over medium coals. Add green beans and soy sauce mixture; toss to coat. Cook 3 to 5 minutes or until heated through, stirring constantly.

BASIL BISCUITS

MAKES 7 BISCUITS

2 cups all-purpose flour

4 tablespoons grated Parmesan cheese, divided

1 tablespoon baking powder

½ teaspoon baking soda

¼ teaspoon salt

4 tablespoons cream cheese

3 tablespoons butter, divided

6 ounces plain yogurt

⅓ cup slivered fresh basil leaves

1 Preheat grilling grid over campfire.

2 Combine flour, 2 tablespoons Parmesan, baking powder, baking soda and salt in large bowl. Cut in cream cheese and 1 tablespoon butter with pastry blender or two knives until mixture forms coarse crumbs. Stir in yogurt and basil, mixing just until dough clings together. Turn dough out onto lightly floured surface; gently pat into a ball. Knead just until dough holds together. Pat and roll dough into 7-inch log. Cut into 7 (1-inch-thick) slices.

3 Melt remaining 2 tablespoons butter. Brush 1 tablespoon butter over bottom of large cast iron skillet. Arrange biscuits in skillet; brush with remaining 1 tablespoon butter. Sprinkle with remaining 2 tablespoons Parmesan.

4 Cover and cook over medium coals 20 to 40 minutes or until golden and firm on top.

MEXICAN-STYLE CORN ON THE COB

MAKES 4 SERVINGS

2 tablespoons mayonnaise

½ teaspoon chili powder

½ teaspoon grated lime peel

4 ears corn, husks and silks removed

2 tablespoons grated Parmesan cheese

1 Preheat grilling grid over campfire. Combine mayonnaise, chili powder and lime peel in small bowl; set aside.

2 Grill corn over medium coals 4 to 6 minutes or until lightly charred, turning 3 times.

3 Immediately spread mayonnaise mixture over corn. Sprinkle with cheese.

ROASTED SWEET POTATOES

MAKES 6 SERVINGS

6 sweet potatoes

Vegetable oil

Optional toppings:
marshmallows, ground
cinnamon, sugar
and/or butter

1 Rub sweet potatoes with oil. Place each potato on 6×6-inch piece of foil. Roll up to seal.

2 Place potatoes around edge of campfire directly on medium coals. Cook 25 minutes or until potatoes are softened. Remove to heatproof surface using large tongs. Let stand until potatoes are cool enough to handle. Top as desired.

BBQ CORN WHEELS

MAKES 4 SERVINGS

4 ears corn on the cob, husked and cleaned

3 red, green or yellow bell peppers, cut into large chunks

¾ cup barbecue sauce

½ cup honey

¼ cup FRENCH'S® Worcestershire Sauce

Vegetable cooking spray

CUT corn into 1-inch slices. Alternately thread corn and pepper chunks onto four metal skewers. (Pierce tip of skewer through center of corn wheel to thread.) Combine barbecue sauce, honey and Worcestershire.

COAT kabobs with vegetable cooking spray. Grill kabobs on greased rack over medium heat for 5 minutes. Cook 5 minutes more until corn is tender, turning and basting with barbecue sauce mixture. Serve any extra sauce on the side with grilled hamburgers, steaks or chicken.

S'More Bananas (page 146)

Chocolate Cake Stuffed Oranges (page 132)

S'More Cones (page 134)

SWEET TREATS

Individual Fruit Pie (page 131)

ple Berry Cinnamon Roll
illet Cobbler (page 152)

INDIVIDUAL FRUIT PIE

MAKES 1 SERVING

1 refrigerated pie crust
(half of a 15-ounce
package) or white
sandwich bread

2 tablespoons butter

¼ cup cherry, apple or
blueberry pie filling

Coarse sugar

1 Cut 1 pie crust into quarters; reserve 2 pieces for another use. Layer 1 tablespoon butter, 1 piece pie crust, cherry pie filling, 1 piece pie crust and 1 tablespoon butter in pie iron. Press tines of fork around edge to crimp.

2 Hold pie iron level over medium coals 6 minutes or until golden brown on each side, turning once. Remove to heatproof surface; carefully remove pie to serving plate. Sprinkle with sugar.

CHOCOLATE CAKE STUFFED ORANGES

MAKES 6 SERVINGS

6 large navel oranges

1 package (about 18 ounces) chocolate cake mix, plus ingredients to prepare mix

1 Slice ½ inch off top of stem end of each orange; reserve tops. Hollow out each orange, leaving ¼ inch of fruit and peel around bottom and sides. Discard fruit or reserve for another use.

2 Place each orange on 8×8-inch piece of foil sprayed with nonstick cooking spray.

3 Prepare cake mix according to package directions. Fill each orange two-thirds full with cake mix; replace tops of oranges slightly off center. Roll foil up and around each orange to seal.

4 Place oranges top side up in medium coals around edge of campfire. Cook 1 hour or until toothpick inserted into centers comes out clean. Remove to heatproof surface using large tongs.

S'MORE CONES

MAKES 4 SERVINGS

4 waffle or sugar cones

½ cup mini marshmallows

½ cup chocolate, white chocolate and/or peanut butter chips

Salted peanuts (optional)

1 Layer each cone evenly with marshmallows, chips and peanuts, if desired. Place each cone on 12×6-inch piece of foil. Roll up to seal.

2 Place cones upright around edge of campfire directly in medium coals. Cook 4 minutes or until lightly toasted. Remove to heatproof surface using large tongs. Let stand until cones are cool enough to handle.

WARM MIXED BERRY PIE
MAKES 8 SERVINGS

2 packages (12 ounces each) frozen mixed berries

⅓ cup sugar

3 tablespoons cornstarch

2 teaspoons grated orange peel

¼ teaspoon ground ginger

1 refrigerated pie crust (half of 15-ounce package)

1 Preheat grilling grid over campfire.

2 Combine berries, sugar, cornstarch, orange peel and ginger in large bowl; toss to coat. Spoon evenly into large cast iron skillet. Roll out pie crust to 12-inch circle. Place over berry mixture; flute edge as desired. Cut slits in top of pie crust to allow steam to escape.

3 Cook 30 minutes over medium coals or until crust is golden brown. Let stand 15 minutes before serving.

EASY GRILLED S'MORES

MAKES 4 SERVINGS

4 sheets (12×8 inches each) REYNOLDS WRAP® Heavy Duty Aluminum Foil

4 whole HONEY MAID® honey graham crackers, broken crosswise in half (8 squares)

2 milk chocolate candy bars (1.55 ounces each), divided in half crosswise

4 JET-PUFFED® Marshmallows

1 Preheat grill to medium. For each s'more, top one graham cracker square with one candy bar half, one marshmallow and another graham cracker square. Repeat with remaining graham crackers, candy and marshmallows.

2 Center one s'more on each sheet of REYNOLDS WRAP® Heavy Duty Aluminum Foil.

3 Bring up foil sides. Double fold top and ends to seal packet, leaving room for heat circulation inside. Repeat to make four packets.

4 Grill 4 to 5 minutes in covered grill. Serve immediately.

APPLES WITH BROWN SUGAR AND CINNAMON

MAKES 4 SERVINGS

2 large apples (Red Delicious, Braeburn or Fuji), cored and sliced into 12 rings

2 tablespoons packed brown sugar

1 tablespoon ground cinnamon

¼ teaspoon ground nutmeg

Caramel or butterscotch sauce, warmed

1 Preheat grilling grid over campfire. Place apples on foil. Combine brown sugar, cinnamon and nutmeg in small bowl. Sprinkle over apple slices; roll up foil to seal.

2 Place apples around edge of campfire directly in medium coals. Cook 10 minutes or until tender and dark golden brown, turning occasionally. Remove to heatproof surface using large tongs. Let stand until apples are cool enough to handle. Drizzle with caramel sauce.

VARIATION

Try peaches wrapped in foil, topped with brown sugar, cinnamon and butter. Cook 8 to 12 minutes or until the fruit is softened.

HOBO-STYLE POPCORN
MAKES 2 SERVINGS

1 tablespoon popcorn
    kernels

1 teaspoon vegetable oil

Butter

Salt and black pepper

1 Place popcorn kernels and oil in center of two 18×18-inch sheets of foil crisscrossed. Bring corners of foil together to make pouch, leaving enough space for popcorn to pop and expand. Pierce top of pouch with long roasting skewer or clean stick.

2 Hold over medium coals of campfire 10 minutes or until popping is 3 seconds or less apart. Remove to heatproof surface. Let stand until cool enough to handle.

3 Top popcorn with butter, salt and pepper.

VARIATIONS
Try different toppings such as chocolate chips, peanut butter chips, Parmesan cheese, marshmallows, peanuts and/or caramel.

DESSERT CRUMBLE

MAKES 4 SERVINGS

1 prepared pie crust

2 tablespoons sugar

1 teaspoon ground cinnamon

4 slices pineapple

1 large peach or nectarine, sliced into 8 wedges

1 large pear, sliced into 8 wedges

8 ounces whipped topping

1 Preheat grilling grid over campfire.

2 Spray metal pie pan with nonstick cooking spray. Place crust in pan, pressing dough onto bottom and up side. Place on grid over medium coals; cook 14 minutes or until golden brown. Set aside to cool.

3 Combine sugar and cinnamon in small bowl. Sprinkle sugar mixture over fruit. Place fruit on grid over medium coals. Grill until golden brown, turning as needed. Fruit should be crisp and slightly firm, not mushy. Transfer to plate; cool slightly. Cut pineapple into bite-size pieces.

4 Break apart crust; divide pieces among four plates. Top with whipped topping and fruit.

S'MORE BANANAS

MAKES 8 SERVINGS

 8 firm bananas, unpeeled

24 miniature marshmallows

 8 tablespoons mini chocolate chips

 8 tablespoons graham cracker crumbs

1 Slice bananas lengthwise halfway through peel and flesh. Place each banana on 12×6-inch piece of foil.

2 Place 3 marshmallows, 1 tablespoon chocolate chips and 1 tablespoon graham cracker crumbs in each banana slit. Roll up and seal foil around each banana.

3 Place wrapped bananas cut side up directly in medium coals around edge of campfire. Cook 40 minutes. Remove to heatproof surface; let stand until cool enough to handle.

CHOCOLATE-PEANUT BUTTER BANANAS

Substitute chocolate syrup, peanut butter and peanuts for the marshmallows, chocolate chips and graham cracker crumbs. Cook as directed. Makes 8 servings.

APPLE CRANBERRY CRUMBLE

MAKES 4 SERVINGS

4 large apples (about 1⅓ pounds), peeled and cut into ¼-inch slices

2 cups fresh or frozen cranberries

⅓ cup granulated sugar

6 tablespoons all-purpose flour, divided

1 teaspoon apple pie spice, divided

¼ teaspoon salt, divided

½ cup chopped walnuts

¼ cup old-fashioned oats

2 tablespoons packed brown sugar

¼ cup (½ stick) butter, cut into small pieces

1 Preheat grilling grid over campfire.

2 Combine apples, cranberries, granulated sugar, 2 tablespoons flour, ½ teaspoon apple pie spice and ⅛ teaspoon salt in large bowl; toss to coat. Spoon into medium cast iron skillet.

3 Combine remaining 4 tablespoons flour, walnuts, oats, brown sugar, remaining ½ teaspoon apple pie spice and ⅛ teaspoon salt in medium bowl; mix well. Cut in butter with pastry blender or two knives until mixture resembles coarse crumbs. Sprinkle over fruit mixture in skillet.

4 Cook 25 to 30 minutes over medium coals or until filling is bubbly and topping is lightly browned.

GRILLED BANANA AND CHOCOLATE PANINI

MAKES 6 SERVINGS

¼ cup (½ stick) butter, softened

1 frozen pound cake (about 10 ounces), thawed and cut into 12 (½-inch-thick) slices

1 cup chocolate-hazelnut spread

3 ripe bananas, cut lengthwise into slices

Ground cinnamon

1 Preheat grilling grid over campfire.

2 Lightly butter one side of each pound cake slice.

3 For each sandwich, lay one slice pound cake, buttered side down, on work surface. Spread chocolate-hazelnut spread over cake slice; top with banana slices and sprinkle with cinnamon. Top with second cake slice, buttered side up.

4 Cook sandwiches over medium coals 1 to 2 minutes per side or until cake is golden brown.

APPLE BERRY CINNAMON ROLL SKILLET COBBLER

MAKES 8 SERVINGS

1 tablespoon cornstarch

2 tablespoons lemon juice

5 apples (about 2 pounds), peeled and cut into ½-inch pieces

½ cup packed brown sugar

¾ teaspoon ground cinnamon

⅛ teaspoon ground ginger

3 tablespoons butter

½ cup coarsely chopped pecans

1 cup fresh blueberries

1 package (13 ounces) refrigerated flaky cinnamon rolls with icing

1 Preheat grilling grid over campfire.

2 Stir cornstarch into lemon juice in large bowl until blended. Add apples, brown sugar, cinnamon and ginger; mix well.

3 Melt butter in large cast iron skillet over medium coals. Add apple mixture and pecans; press into single layer to cover bottom of skillet. Sprinkle with blueberries.

4 Cook 20 minutes. Separate cinnamon rolls; reserve icing. Arrange cinnamon rolls over warm fruit mixture.

5 Cook 20 to 25 minutes or until filling is bubbly and cinnamon rolls are deep golden brown. Drizzle with icing. Let stand 5 minutes before serving.

INDEX

Cast Iron *(continued)*

Chicken Noodle Soup, 60

Chorizo Hash, 32

Classic Hash Browns, 21

Crispy Skillet Potatoes, 16

Easy Vegetable Beef Stew, 56

Fajitas, 86

Fish Tacos, 76

Ham and Barbecued Bean Skillet, 88

Mexican Casserole with Tortilla Chips, 96

Nutty Pan-Fried Trout, 94

Pizza Casserole, 69

Sausage and Cheddar Corn Bread, 26

Sausage and Peppers, 92

Sawmill Biscuits and Gravy, 30

Skillet Mac and Cheese, 112

Southern Fried Catfish with Hush Puppies, 72

Sweet Potato and Turkey Sausage Hash, 28

Tangy Red Cabbage with Apples and Bacon, 108

Walking Tacos, 80

Warmed Mixed Berry Pie, 136

Whole Wheat Pancakes, 24

Chicken

All-American Barbecue Grilled Chicken, 75

BBQ Chicken Skillet Pizza, 100

Cajun BBQ Beer Can Chicken, 82

Chicken and Fruit Kabobs, 98

Chicken Noodle Soup, 60

Fajitas, 86

Grilled Buffalo Chicken Wraps, 58

Southwestern Chicken Soup, 50

Chicken and Fruit Kabobs, 98

Chicken Noodle Soup, 60

Chili

Classic Chili, 46

Corn Chip Chili, 38

Chocolate

Chocolate Cake Stuffed Oranges, 132

Chocolate-Peanut Butter Bananas, 146

Easy Grilled S'mores, 138

Grilled Banana and Chocolate Panini, 150

S'more Bananas, 146

S'more Cones, 134

Chocolate Cake Stuffed Oranges, 132

Chocolate-Peanut Butter Bananas, 146

Chorizo Hash, 32

Classic Chili, 46

Classic Hash Browns, 21

Corn

Bacon-Wrapped Roasted Corn, 105

BBQ Corn Wheels, 126

Mexican-Style Corn on the Cob, 122

Southwestern Chicken Soup, 50

Corn Chip Chili, 38

Crispy Skillet Potatoes, 16

D

Dessert Crumble, 144

Dough, Refrigerated

Apple Berry Cinnamon Roll Skillet Cobbler, 152

Biscuit-Wrapped Sausages, 7

Breakfast Biscuit Bake, 12

Individual Fruit Pie, 131

Twisted Cinnamon Biscuits, 22

Warmed Mixed Berry Pie, 136

METRIC CONVERSION CHART

VOLUME MEASUREMENTS (dry)

1/8 teaspoon = 0.5 mL
1/4 teaspoon = 1 mL
1/2 teaspoon = 2 mL
3/4 teaspoon = 4 mL
1 teaspoon = 5 mL
1 tablespoon = 15 mL
2 tablespoons = 30 mL
1/4 cup = 60 mL
1/3 cup = 75 mL
1/2 cup = 125 mL
2/3 cup = 150 mL
3/4 cup = 175 mL
1 cup = 250 mL
2 cups = 1 pint = 500 mL
3 cups = 750 mL
4 cups = 1 quart = 1 L

VOLUME MEASUREMENTS (fluid)

1 fluid ounce (2 tablespoons) = 30 mL
4 fluid ounces (1/2 cup) = 125 mL
8 fluid ounces (1 cup) = 250 mL
12 fluid ounces (1 1/2 cups) = 375 mL
16 fluid ounces (2 cups) = 500 mL

WEIGHTS (mass)

1/2 ounce = 15 g
1 ounce = 30 g
3 ounces = 90 g
4 ounces = 120 g
8 ounces = 225 g
10 ounces = 285 g
12 ounces = 360 g
16 ounces = 1 pound = 450 g

DIMENSIONS

1/16 inch = 2 mm
1/8 inch = 3 mm
1/4 inch = 6 mm
1/2 inch = 1.5 cm
3/4 inch = 2 cm
1 inch = 2.5 cm

OVEN TEMPERATURES

250°F = 120°C
275°F = 140°C
300°F = 150°C
325°F = 160°C
350°F = 180°C
375°F = 190°C
400°F = 200°C
425°F = 220°C
450°F = 230°C

BAKING PAN SIZES

Utensil	Size in Inches/Quarts	Metric Volume	Size in Centimeters
Baking or Cake Pan (square or rectangular)	8×8×2	2 L	20×20×5
	9×9×2	2.5 L	23×23×5
	12×8×2	3 L	30×20×5
	13×9×2	3.5 L	33×23×5
Loaf Pan	8×4×3	1.5 L	20×10×7
	9×5×3	2 L	23×13×7
Round Layer Cake Pan	8×1½	1.2 L	20×4
	9×1½	1.5 L	23×4
Pie Plate	8×1¼	750 mL	20×3
	9×1¼	1 L	23×3
Baking Dish or Casserole	1 quart	1 L	—
	1½ quart	1.5 L	—
	2 quart	2 L	—